DR. MYLES MUNROE

KEYS *for* PRAYER

WHITAKER
HOUSE

KEYS FOR PRAYER

ISBN-13: 978-1-60374-031-9
ISBN-10: 1-60374-031-7
Printed in the United States of America
© 2008 by Dr. Myles Munroe

Whitaker House
1030 Hunt Valley Circle
New Kensington, PA 15068
www.whitakerhouse.com

Library of Congress Cataloging-in-Publication Data

Munroe, Myles.
  Keys for prayer / Myles Munroe.
      p. cm.
  Summary: "Inspirational quotations on the topic of prayer gleaned from the Bible and Myles Munroe's teachings on the subject"—Provided by publisher.
  ISBN-13: 978-1-60374-031-9 (pbk. : alk. paper) ISBN-10: 1-60374-031-7
  1. Prayer—Christianity. 2. Prayer—Biblical teaching. I. Title.
  BV210.3.M83 2008
  248.3'2—dc22
                              2007044808

3 4 5 6 7 8 9 10 11 12 **ᴜ** 16 15 14 13 12 11 10 09

INTRODUCTION

To understand prayer, you must first understand the purpose of the Creator. Prayer is a result of God's established authority structure between heaven and earth, as well as a product of His faithfulness to His Word. This is because prayer was born out of man's God-given assignment. The Creator said, *"Let them rule...over all the earth"* (Genesis 1:26). His design is for human beings to call upon Him to fulfill His Word *"on earth as it is in heaven"* (Matthew 6:10). God's commitment to His Word is the basis of the prayer principle. He is faithful to fulfill His promises and decrees because of His integrity or holiness.

Through *Keys to Prayer*, you can begin a dynamic new prayer life based on your assignment from God. You will not only learn about prayer, but you will also know how to pray—and receive results!

—*Dr. Myles Munroe*

*P*rayer is man exercising his
God-given, legal authority on earth
to invoke heaven's influence on the world.
In other words, prayer is earthly license
for heavenly interference.

*J*ohn Wesley once said,
"God does nothing but in answer to prayer."
Prayer is not an option for mankind
but a necessity.

*S*ecretly, we wonder, "Does God *really* hear me when I pray?" or "Why is prayer so boring and fruitless for me?"

There's a strong connection between underdeveloped, defeated, or directionless lives and confusion over prayer.

$\mathscr{P}$rayer is meant to be answered—or else God would not ask us to pray. He isn't interested in wasting your time and efforts. He is too practical for that.

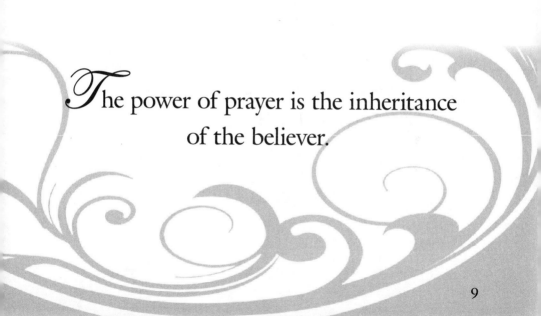

The power of prayer is the inheritance
of the believer.

$\mathscr{P}$rayer is not just an activity, ritual, or obligation. Nor is it begging God to do what we want. It is communion and communication with God that touches His heart.

When you understand the principles
of prayer, you will begin
to communicate with God
with power, grace, and confidence.

$\mathscr{P}$rayer has the power to…
- transform lives
- change circumstances
- give peace and perseverance in the midst of trial
- alter the course of nations
- win the world for Christ

KEYS for PRAYER

$\mathcal{G}$od is faithful to answer prayer.
Every prayer based on God's Word and
offered in faith by someone in right
relationship with Him *is answered*.

*G*od answers as soon as we ask, and He reveals those answers in His timing. Jesus told His disciples *"that they should always pray and not give up"* (Luke 18:1).

*J*esus expected His prayers to be heard. He said, *"Father, I thank you that you have heard me. I knew that you always hear me"* (John 11:41–42).

We must know how to approach God and learn the kind of prayers He responds to. We must pray as Jesus prayed.

*J*esus said, *"Therefore I tell you, whatever you ask for in prayer, believe that you have received it, and it will be yours"* (Mark 11:24). The answer is so sure that we are instructed to believe it has already happened.

$\mathcal{T}$rue prayer…

- builds intimacy with God
- brings honor to His nature and character
- causes respect for His integrity
- enables belief in His Word
- produces trust in His love
- affirms His purposes
- appropriates His promises

18

*G*od said, *"Let us make man in our image, in our likeness, and let them rule over all the earth"* (Genesis 1:26). Amazingly, man was created not only to have a relationship with God, but also to share His authority.

The relationship of love God established with mankind is not separate from the purpose God has for mankind. Rather, the relationship is foundational to the purpose; both are essential keys to prayer.

$\mathcal{W}$e can function in the purposes for which we were created only as we are connected to our Source. God doesn't want man to work *for* Him but *with* Him. The Bible says that we are *"God's fellow workers"* (2 Corinthians 6:1).

When Adam and Eve broke relationship with God by rebelling against Him, their effectiveness in prayer was also broken. True prayer is maintained through oneness of heart and purpose with God. Only then can we fulfill His ways and plans.

When we pray, we represent God's interests on earth, and representation requires relationship.

*T*he heart of prayer is twofold:

- Prayer is an expression of mankind's unity and relationship of love with God.

- Prayer is an expression of mankind's affirmation of and participation in God's purposes for the earth.

$\mathscr{P}$rayer means union with God—unity and singleness of purpose, thought, desire, will, reason, motive, objective, and feelings. God causes things to happen on earth when men and women are in agreement with His will.

$\mathcal{W}$hether we are praying for individual, family, community, national, or world needs, we must seek to be in agreement with God's will. God's plan is for man to ask Him to accomplish His purposes in the world so that goodness and truth may reign rather than evil and darkness. This is the essence of exercising dominion.

KEYS for PRAYER

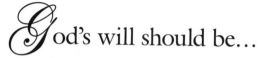

God's will should be…

- the backbone of your prayers
- the heart of your intercession
- the source of your confidence
  in supplication
- the strength of your fervent,
  effectual prayers

$\mathscr{P}$raying does not mean convincing God to do your will, but rather doing His will through your will.

All that God is, and all that He has, may
be received through prayer.

29

$\mathscr{P}$rayer should not be open-ended. It should be purpose-driven, motivated by a knowledge of God's ways and intentions.

$\mathcal{T}$he key to effective prayer is understanding God's purpose for your life, His reason for your existence—as a human being in general and as an individual specifically.

*Y*our purpose should be the "raw material" or foundational matter of your prayer life. Prayer is calling forth what God has already purposed and predestined— continuing His work of creation and the establishment of His plans for the earth.

*I*f we ask God for things that are contrary to our purpose, we will be frustrated. Jesus' assurance in prayer was based on knowing and doing God's will. He always prayed for God's will to be done and then worked to accomplish it.

When we stop praying, we allow
God's purposes for the world to be hindered,
and we leave people susceptible to the
influences of Satan and sin.

$\mathcal{T}$ime spent in prayer is not time wasted
but time invested.

*I*f you do not pray, God will find someone who will agree with His plans. Yet you will fail to fulfill *your* role in His purposes. God does not want you to miss out on this privilege. *"You do not have, because you do not ask God"* (James 4:2).

God did not change His purposes when mankind fell, because His purposes are eternal. Christ Jesus became the Second Adam. He redeemed mankind so we could be fully restored to a relationship of love with God and participation in His purposes for the earth.

To restore God's purpose, Christ had to be a Representative of the legal authority of the earth—man. He had to come to earth as a human being, as the beginning of a new family of mankind who would be devoted to God—*the firstborn among many brothers* (Romans 8:29).

*J*esus has the right to reign and ask God to intervene in the world because He was the perfect Man and Sacrifice. His prayers for mankind are powerful. *"He is able to save completely those who come to God through him, because he always lives to intercede for them"* (Hebrews 7:25).

$\mathscr{T}$here is a vital relationship between redemption and true prayer. The position and authority Jesus won have been transferred back to mankind through spiritual rebirth in Christ. Only through Christ's redemption are we restored to our purposes, and only through Christ do we have the right to pray to God with authority.

$\mathscr{B}$ecause Jesus gave believers the Holy Spirit, we can agree with God's purposes even when we are uncertain about how to pray. *"We do not know what we ought to pray for, but the Spirit himself intercedes for us with groans that words cannot express"* (Romans 8:26).

41

*B*ecause Jesus delivered us from Satan's dominion, Satan no longer has authority over us. Rather, we have authority over him in the name of Jesus.

The authority of Jesus' name gives us access to our heavenly Father. It enables us to agree with Him and His purposes, and to ask Him to fulfill His Word as He meets our needs and the needs of others.

$\mathscr{P}$ower in prayer is not based on emotions, feelings, or the theories of men, but upon the Word of God, *"which lives and abides forever"* (1 Peter 1:23 NKJV). Prayer is joining forces with God the Father by calling attention to His promises.

As the Son of Man, Jesus kept a close relationship with the Father through prayer. He did what God directed Him to do and what He saw God actively working to accomplish in the world. He relied on the grace and Spirit of God. We can do the same.

$\mathcal{F}$rom Genesis to Revelation, God always found a human being to help Him accomplish His purposes. He comes to you now and asks, in effect, "Are you willing? Will you help Me fulfill My purposes for your life and for the earth?"

$\mathscr{G}$od says the church is
"a royal priesthood" (1 Peter 2:9).
In God's presence, we can commune with
Him, offer effectual prayer, and be His
mediators on behalf of the world.

Because we know God is holy, we can believe He will fulfill what He has promised. We can believe we will receive what we ask of Him according to His Word.

A cardinal principle of answered prayer is belief in the trustworthiness of the One to whom you're praying. The power of your prayers depends on it.

49

$\mathcal{D}$ouble-mindedness is the opposite of holiness. If you tell God you believe Him but act in the opposite way, then you are not integrated, pure, holy. You are double-minded. *"That man should not think he will receive anything from the Lord"* (James 1:7).

KEYS for PRAYER

We prepare to enter the presence of God by first asking ourselves, "Am I in a position to approach God in holiness? Have I thought, said, or done things that are contrary to His Word and law of love?"

$\mathcal{W}$e must accept Christ's sacrifice for our sins, repent from wrongdoing, and make clean the secret closets of sin and disobedience within us so we can be effective in prayer. *"Your sins have hidden [God's] face from you, so that he will not hear"* (Isaiah 59:2).

We need to be cleansed continually so we can live before God in holiness—the holiness Christ died to provide for us. *"If we confess our sins, he is faithful and just and will forgive us our sins and purify us from all unrighteousness"* (1 John 1:9).

$\mathcal{G}$od wants to bless us and answer our prayers. That is why He tells us to deal with our sins. When your sins are forgiven and you are right with God, you can genuinely fellowship with Him and with other believers—and that brings the power of agreement in prayer.

You need to make sure you are in the Word when you come before God—that you've *read* the Word, that the Word is *in* you, that you are *obeying* the Word. Otherwise, you will enter God's presence with your own ideas and attitudes.

*W*e prepare for prayer by separating ourselves from our normal environment and activities. When you are seeking God, you can't be around distractions.

$\mathcal{I}$f you're going to seek God, you have to be serious about it. God says, "If you want to find Me, you will do so only *when you seek Me with all your heart*" (Jeremiah 29:13).

*A*fter you have taken the appropriate
steps to enter God's presence, then you can
"present your requests to God"
(Philippians 4:6).

We have to remain in a state of preparedness for prayer. We aren't to approach God in an offhand or careless way. It is important to learn what it means to honor the Lord and reflect His nature and character in our lives.

$\mathscr{I}$f we are going to do any kind of business with God, we need to be able to function in the faith the Bible speaks of. *"Without faith it is impossible to please God"* (Hebrews 11:6).

*M*en and women were created in God's image to operate in the same way He does—through words of faith. *"For he spoke, and it came to be; he commanded, and it stood firm"* (Psalm 33:9).

*G*od created by believing in the reality of what He would create. When you ask for something in prayer based on God's Word, you must start speaking about it as if it already exists. Moreover, you have to *keep on* speaking about it in this way in order to see its manifestation.

$\mathscr{S}$ome answers to prayer have not manifested because it is not yet their season. Between the seed prayer and the manifestation of the fruit, stay reading, meditating on, speaking, and living the Word of God so it can flow continuously into your life. To keep believing, keep taking in the Word.

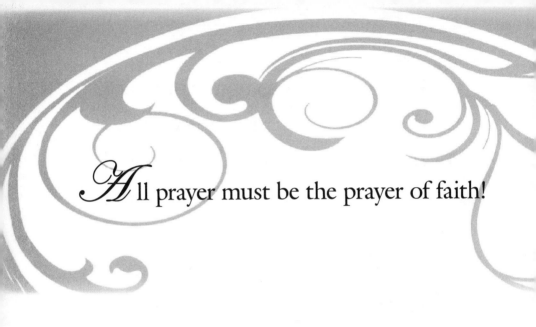

*A*ll prayer must be the prayer of faith!

*J*esus cast out demons with just a word. He'd say, "Come out," and they would leave. This process took only seconds, yet in the morning, He had spent hours praying. Jesus wants us to operate as He operated: much time in communion with the Father, and much accomplished for the kingdom.

Prayer saves you time. We can never really be too busy to pray because prayer makes our lives more focused, efficient, and peaceful.

$\mathcal{W}$e often sing, "This is the day that the Lord has made." I imagine God is saying to us, "If this is My day, then why don't you come and talk to Me about it?"

*H*ours with God make minutes with men effective.

Prayer gives you discernment you wouldn't otherwise have. God tells you what is truly important, compared to what seems urgent. He tells you what you should and shouldn't do now. He gives you wisdom to address your situation. Prayer enables you to think clearly and wisely.

$\mathcal{W}$hy did Jesus spend hours in prayer? It is because He had a genuine relationship with the Father, and any relationship takes time to build and maintain.

*W*e often discover that when we spend time in prayer, God begins to use *us* to change circumstances.

*M*any people are waiting for a "burning bush" experience or the appearance of an angel. They don't hear from God because they're waiting in the wrong way. God doesn't usually speak out loud. That's not intimate enough. He speaks directly to our spirits. God communicates to us through thoughts, ideas, impressions, and discernment.

*J*esus prayed by Himself to teach us that prayer is a personal and private relationship and responsibility. Corporate prayer should never be a substitute for personal and private time with the Father.

The Lord's Prayer is a *model* for prayer. In other words, you don't need to repeat the words of this prayer exactly; instead, you should use them as a pattern.

$\mathscr{P}$raying *"Our Father"* (Luke 11:2 NKJV)
means that when we approach God,
we are to bring other people's concerns
with us. Our prayers are selfish
if we don't also pray for others.

We are to address God as Father, going to Him with the awareness and confession that He is the Source who can provide for the needs of everyone. Whatever your problem, the Father has the answer.

When you pray, *"Our Father **in heaven**"* (Luke 11:2 NKJV), you're saying to God, "I recognize I need help from outside my realm." It is a confession of submission.

*H*allowed *be Your name*" (Luke 11:2 NKJV). The word *hallowed* means reverenced, set apart, or sanctified. We are to worship the Father as the Holy One. Sometimes we try to bypass this step and get right into prayer. God is saying to us, "Honor My name first." We can make our requests later, but we begin with worship.

When you pray, honor all the attributes of God's holiness, such as His love, faithfulness, integrity, and grace. After you pray, continue to honor Him in your life and in all your interactions with others.

Your kingdom come. Your will be done on earth as it is in heaven" (Luke 11:2 NKJV). A true person of prayer is not interested in his own kingdom. He is interested in God's kingdom and what He wants accomplished. God is delighted when you are excited about the things He's excited about.

You don't have to worry about having your needs met if you start praying for God's will to be done in other people's lives. God will bless you because He will see that you have aligned your will with His will, that you are reaching out to others in love and compassion.

$\mathscr{G}$ive **us** *day by day our daily bread*" (Luke 11:3 NKJV). When you ask for bread, you have to ask for bread for everybody. We normally say, "Lord, provide for me." Yet God tells us, "Ask for others as well as yourself. Pray for others."

And forgive us our sins, for we also forgive everyone who is indebted to us" (Luke 11:4 NKJV). Are you holding anything against anyone? Does anyone have anything against you? Don't expect to have your prayers answered if you refuse to forgive others. Having good relationships is one of the keys to answered prayer.

$\mathcal{D}$o not lead us into temptation, but deliver us from the evil one" (Luke 11:4 NKJV). This doesn't mean God might steer us toward temptation against our wills. It means we are to ask Him for wisdom so we won't put ourselves into situations that will cause us to compromise our relationship with Him.

For Yours is the kingdom and the power and the glory forever. Amen" (Matthew 6:13 NKJV). After you have prayed, worship the Father again. This acknowledges to Him, "I know You're going to answer this prayer; therefore, I'm going to thank You ahead of time and give You all the glory for what happens."

The Bible says, *"Be still, and know that I am God"* (Psalm 46:10). In this sense, prayer is the expression of man's dependency upon God for all things.

We are usually distracted by many things when we pray. Our minds are elsewhere. You therefore need to put yourself in a position where you can become quiet, collect yourself—your thoughts, attention, and concentration—and let the Lord calm your heart. Silence helps bring you into a unity of heart and purpose with God.

After silence, we should give God adoration. When you adore someone, you express how precious that person is to you. We are to worship God for who He is: King of all the earth, our Creator, our Savior, our All in All.

Confession follows silence and adoration in prayer. Most of us have been taught that confession means bringing up our past sins, feeling remorse, getting emotional, and so on. That's not the heart of confession. Confession means agreeing with God about what He says *to* you and *about* you.

Confession takes place when God points out something in your life and says, "Get rid of that" or "You know you shouldn't have done that," and you say, "Yes, God, You're right. I won't do that any longer." Then you put your trust in Him to enable you to walk by the Spirit.

Keys for Prayer

King David committed adultery, conceived a child out of wedlock, and killed a man. So why did God say that David was *"a man after His own heart"* (1 Samuel 13:14 NKJV)? David was completely honest about his transgressions. He didn't make excuses; he admitted that he had sinned against God. This made his prayer life powerful.

*I*f you have done something wrong, confess it quickly. Agree with God, ask for forgiveness, and go on with your life.

*I*f you have confessed before God, then your heart is right, and you can offer a *"sacrifice of praise"* (Hebrews 13:15) to Him. You can give thanks abundantly because your heart is free.

Supplication implies three things. It means to intercede, to petition, and to brood. Brooding means a deep passion. When you offer supplication, you feel the heart of God. You desire His will so much that it becomes an emotional experience.

*P*rayer is a very intentional communication. It is an art. You need to address God specifically for your particular petitions. If you want peace, you appeal to Him as *Jehovah-Shalom* (The Lord Our Peace) rather than *Jehovah-Jireh* (The Lord Our Provider). If you need healing, you address Him as *Jehovah-Rapha* (The Lord Our Healer).

$\mathscr{W}$rite down the things you want to pray for; then, next to those items, write down the Scriptures you're going to use when you pray. You will be praying according to God's Word, and God will send help for each request.

$\mathscr{P}$leading your case before God does not mean begging and moaning. It is something you do because you rightfully deserve what you are asking for based on God's promises.

$\mathcal{G}$od wants you to come to prayer with an attitude that says, "You're the only One who can help me." Often, we pray for God's help, but we have a backup plan, just in case. We need to depend completely on Him.

KEYS for PRAYER

*A*fter you plead your case, then believe. Asking, in itself, doesn't cause you to receive. When you start doubting, be honest, like the father of the demon-possessed boy, and say, *"Lord, I believe; help my unbelief!"* (Mark 9:24 NKJV). We can't let doubt enter into our prayers. It will short-circuit them.

*I*f you truly believe that when you prayed, you received what you asked for, then you will start thanking God. We are not to wait until we see the manifestation of our answers before expressing our gratitude.

$\mathcal{P}$ractice active belief that shows you are living in expectation of the answer to your prayer by making preparations to receive it. *"Ask and it will be given to you; seek and you will find; knock and the door will be opened to you"* (Luke 11:9). No barrier can stop what God has for you.

*L*earning about prayer but not practicing it is a hurdle to answered prayer. We think it's a part of our lives, but it hasn't made it from our heads to our hearts, from theory to practice. The best approach to prayer is *to pray*.

*M*ental assent *agrees* with God but does not *believe* God. The only way God's promises will become a reality in your life is for you to act on them—and you can't act on them without faith.

$\mathcal{W}$e are trained and conditioned to live by our five senses alone. If we cannot analyze something and empirically conclude that it works, we do not believe it is real. Yet faith is the substance and evidence of things that our sense knowledge cannot see.

We must internalize the Word if it is going to make an impact on our lives. Let it truly sink into your spirit. Turn it over in your mind in order to understand its truths and implications and then apply it to your life. This is how the Word of God becomes the means for answered prayer.

$\mathcal{H}$ope that is focused only on the afterlife can become a hurdle to answered prayer. God wants to give us blessings in this life. If we think God's blessings are all in the future, we will not exercise faith to see their fulfillment now. Where faith is not applied, fulfillment cannot be given.

Keys for Prayer

God's blessings have already been accomplished in the spiritual realm. He is waiting for a human to believe Him so He can release them. Jesus said, *"According to your faith will it be done to you"* (Matthew 9:29).

When we exhibit wishful thinking and doubt, we show that we are skeptical about God's character and integrity. Doubt is really an insult to God. No wonder James said that if a person doubts, *"that man should not think he will receive anything from the Lord"* (James 1:7).

*I*t is not the size of your faith that counts—it is the size of your God.

When a person doesn't want to bother
with prayer because he feels he has more
important things to do, or when he allows
the many concerns of this life to crowd out
the practice of prayer, then whatever he
does know about prayer will not bear
any fruit in his life.

There is now no condemnation" (Romans 8:1). This truth is crucial for us to understand if we are to approach God in prayer. God has forgiven and forgotten your sin if you have confessed it, repented of it, and believed that it is covered by the blood of Jesus.

$\mathcal{S}$ome people are hindered in prayer because they don't believe they are worthy enough to receive an answer. We should treat ourselves with respect and approach God as His children, who have been given *"the riches of God's grace"* (Ephesians 1:7). He has made you a co-heir with His Son. Therefore, live and pray accordingly.

You do not receive, because you ask with wrong motives, that you may spend what you get on your pleasures" (James 4:3).

Are you praying for something just to promote your own selfish purposes? Or are you asking God to fulfill His Word so His kingdom can come on the earth?

113

$\mathscr{B}$roken relationships in the home
will hinder your prayers. If we do not
demonstrate the love, compassion,
forgiveness, and grace of God to others, we
are misrepresenting Him. How can we ask
Him to fulfill His purposes by answering
our prayers when we are violating those very
purposes by the way we treat others?

Keys for Prayer

God will not answer our prayers if we are seeking idols. This means not only statues, but also idols of the heart. An idol is anything we give higher priority than God. He deserves our primary love, respect, and devotion.

An ungenerous heart can hinder your prayers. Proverbs 21:13 says, *"If a man shuts his ears to the cry of the poor, he too will cry out and not be answered."*

Prayer is actually very simple. It is speaking the Word to God exactly as He gave it to us.

$\mathcal{O}$ur power in prayer is the Word of God. Our job is to learn how to handle it properly and responsibly. This can make the difference between answered and unanswered prayer. We can use God's Word correctly only when we understand what it is and how to apply it.

*G*od Himself is speaking in the Word, because the Word is who He is. *"In the beginning was the Word, and the Word was with God, and the **Word was God**"* (John 1:1). Therefore, God's presence becomes a part of our prayers when we speak His Word in faith.

119

The power of God's Word is so great that, as Jesus said, if our faith is the size of a mustard seed, mountains can be moved.

*G*od is a God of the Word. He says, *"My Word...will not return to me empty, but will accomplish what I desire and achieve the purpose for which I sent it"* (Isaiah 55:11). If the church would believe this Scripture, it would shake the world.

$\mathcal{T}$here are two conditions to answered prayer: Jesus said, ***"If you abide in Me, and My words abide in you***, *you will ask what you desire, and it shall be done for you"* (John 15:7 NKJV).

KEYS for PRAYER

What does it mean for you to abide in Jesus? It means to constantly flow in spiritual communion with Him. You do this by fellowshipping with Him, worshipping Him, praying, and fasting.

What does it mean to have Jesus' words living in you? The Word is truly inside us when it directs our thoughts and actions. What's the first thing that comes out of your mouth when you are under pressure? Is it an affirmation of faith? Or is it fear, frustration, doubt, or anger?

*J*esus gave the condition, *"If...My words abide in you..."* (John 15:7 NKJV) so the last part of the verse having to do with prayer could be fulfilled: *"...ask what you desire, and it shall be done for you."* If His words are in you, what you ask for will reflect those words.

The Word is powerful because it produces in us what pleases God and causes Him to respond to our requests—*faith*.

*I*f you have faith in God's Word, He will take what is "impossible" and make it seem like an everyday thing. Sometimes He will take away all your other alternatives because He wants to show you His miracle-working power. If the Word is all you have to go on, you're about to receive a miracle!

When you pray God's Word in faith, things that have been bound up will suddenly open up. You will say, "But I had been trying to accomplish that for ten years!" Yes, but you hadn't prayed according to God's Word until now. Belief will open doors that hard work cannot unlock.

You can be sure God always hears your prayers—one hundred percent of the time—when you pray according to His will.

The Bible is filled with stories of the power of God to save, heal, and bless. These accounts are God's faith messages to us, telling us that He will intervene on our behalf, also.

When we wholeheartedly embrace the Word, it will keep our lives in line with God's will so that nothing will hinder us from walking in His ways and receiving answers to our prayers.

*J*esus' name is not a magic formula that guarantees automatic acceptance of our prayers. We're not effective in prayer just by using the word *Jesus,* but by understanding the significance of who He is and appropriating His power through faith in His name. It's not the name, but what the name represents, that makes the difference.

No one can claim power through Jesus' name without having official child-of-God status. The authority we have in His name through prayer is a covenantal authority; it is based on our covenant relationship with God through Jesus Christ.

$\mathcal{W}$e must be able to legally use the authority behind the power of Jesus' name to obtain results in prayer. The Father asks, "Are you praying based on Christ's righteousness or on your own merits? Do you understand who My Son is? Do you believe in His authority and power?"

*J*esus alone can be your legal channel to the Father. *"For there is one God and one mediator between God and men, the man Christ Jesus"* (1 Timothy 2:5).

Jesus, meaning "Savior," is the name of Christ in His humanity because He came to earth to accomplish the salvation of the world. *I Am* is the name of Christ in His divinity because Jesus is the revelation of God in human form. Since He is the I Am, His attributes are as numerous as your needs—and beyond!

When you give someone power of attorney, that person has the legal authority to speak for you and do business in your name. Praying in the name of Jesus is giving Him power of attorney to intercede on your behalf when you make requests of the Father.

*J*esus is actively working on our behalf, representing our interests to God: *"Therefore he is able to save completely those who come to God through him, because he always lives to intercede for them"* (Hebrews 7:25). If the Son is representing you, then you don't have to worry about your requests being heard by the Father.

*J*esus gave us the Holy Spirit, who assists in exercising power of attorney and enables us to pray. *"The Spirit intercedes for the saints in accordance with God's will"* (Romans 8:27). *"Pray in the Spirit on all occasions with all kinds of prayers and requests"* (Ephesians 6:18).

*P*rayer and fasting are equal parts of a single ministry. Jesus said, *"**When you pray…**"* and *"**When you fast…**"* (Matthew 6:5, 16). Just as prayer is not an option for the believer, fasting is not an option. It is a natural expectation of God for His people.

A fast is a conscious, intentional decision to abstain for a time from the pleasure of eating in order to gain vital spiritual benefits.

The Holy Spirit may move upon a person or group and give them a desire to fast. Yet most of the time, fasting is an act of our faith and our wills. It is a decision we make based on our obedience to Christ and our love for Him.

Fasting is a point of intimacy with God. It means putting God first, focusing your attention on Him alone—not on His blessings, but on God Himself—and giving your whole heart to Him in prayer. It shows Him you love and appreciate Him. It is setting yourself apart and seeking God rather than your own interests.

*F*asting is not a matter of trying to get something *from* God. It's a matter of trying to get *to* God.

Fasting does not change God; it changes us—and it transforms our prayers.

$\mathcal{G}$od reveals Himself only to people who want to know Him. *"You will seek me and find me when you seek me with all your heart"* (Jeremiah 29:13). When you find God Himself, you will discover that everything you need comes with Him.

$\mathscr{F}$asting fosters a sensitive environment for the working of prayer. It enables us to see the fulfillment of God's Word and purposes for us as individuals and as the body of Christ.

The main purpose of fasting is to benefit others. It is a form of intercession. Fasting often brings breakthroughs in difficult circumstances or in the lives of those who are resistant to the gospel.

Fasting enables you to increase your spiritual capacity. It exerts discipline over your physical appetites, bringing them under subjection to what your spirit desires. Your body begins to obey your spirit rather than its own impulses and habits. The body becomes a servant of the Lord, rather than the master of your spirit.

Fasting is emptying ourselves of food and filling ourselves with God. It allows us to receive guidance, wisdom, instruction, and knowledge from Him. We receive revelation from God we can't receive otherwise.

$\mathcal{F}$asting enables us to receive the
fullness of God's power for ministry.
Sometimes prayer alone is not enough to
accomplish His purposes. You may need
to add a spirit of consecration to God and
abstain from what can interfere with the
flow of His power in your life.

*A*lthough you received the Holy Spirit when you were born again, a fast will ignite His power within you. Your love for the Father will be renewed. It will be a joy to witness to others about God's love and grace. You will be able to serve God in ways you never expected.

Keys for Prayer

*T*he absolute necessity of prayer must be like an indelible image upon our hearts and minds. If we want to see God's will done on earth, we must do our part—we must *pray*. God desires you to partner with Him in the great purpose of reclaiming and redeeming the world.

Prayer is a sacred trust from God and the most important activity of humanity.

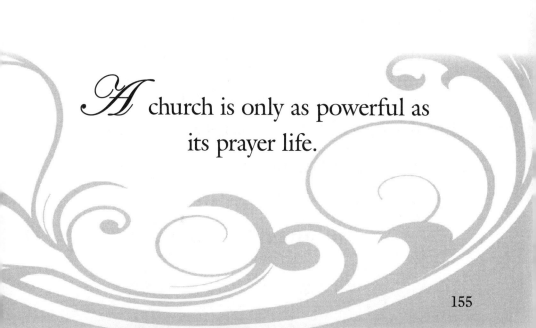

A church is only as powerful as its prayer life.

Prayer is the greatest opportunity and privilege offered to a person in Christ. It is for the *entire* body of Christ—not just an elite group of "intercessory prayer warriors." All of us have the power to bring God's will on earth so the world can be healed and transformed by His grace.

*U*se the purpose and position God has given you to invite heaven to intervene on earth. Prepare your heart, mind, soul, and strength to agree that God's will be done until *"the kingdom of the world has become the kingdom of our Lord and of his Christ"* (Revelation 11:15). Become a person of prayer.

ABOUT THE AUTHOR

*D*r. Myles Munroe is an international motivational speaker, best-selling author, educator, leadership mentor, and consultant for government and business. Traveling extensively throughout the world, Dr. Munroe addresses critical issues affecting the full range of human, social, and spiritual development. The central theme of his message is the transformation of followers into leaders and the maximization of individual potential.

Founder and president of Bahamas Faith Ministries International (BFMI), a multidimensional organization headquartered in Nassau, Bahamas, Dr. Munroe is also the founder and executive producer of a number of radio and television programs aired worldwide. He has a B.A. from Oral Roberts University, an M.A. from the University of Tulsa, and has been awarded a number of honorary doctoral degrees.

Dr. Munroe and his wife, Ruth, travel as a team and are involved in teaching seminars together. Both are leaders who minister with sensitive hearts and international vision. They are the proud parents of two college graduates, Charisa and Chairo (Myles, Jr.).

Nicole Mansford

THE ISLANDS OF THE
bahamas

For Information on Religious Tourism
e-mail: ljohnson@bahamas.com
1.800.224.3681

www.worship.bahamas.com

These inspirational quotes from best-selling author Dr. Myles Munroe on leadership, single living, marriage, and prayer can be applied to your life in powerful and practical ways.

Keys for Leadership: ISBN: 978-1-60374-029-6 • Gift • 160 pages
Keys for Living Single: ISBN: 978-1-60374-032-6 • Gift • 160 pages
Keys for Marriage: ISBN: 978-1-60374-030-2 • Gift • 160 pages
Keys for Prayer: ISBN: 978-1-60374-031-9 • Gift • 160 pages

WHITAKER
HOUSE